A CHILD'S CHRISTMAS CO

THE DENVER ART MUSEUM

TABLE OF CONTENTS

SANTA'S SNACK

Make a sturdy sandwich of rye bread, cheese and ham, or whatever Mother has in the house.

On a cold winter's night, hot tea or mulled cider tastes good. Heat, but do not boil, apple juice or cider. Pour it in a mug. Add a clove and a cinnamon stick.

Christmas cookies for dessert. (See page 34.)

Maybe you'd better make two sandwiches.

Santa's Route.

SURPRISE FOR GRANDMAMA

When Grandmama comes visiting, show her you've been thinking of her. Surprise her. Make something special. Scones can be made ahead of time. Suppose Grandmama comes early and surprises *you*. Serve bread and butter sandwiches, tea or coffee.

Remember — with a little love, everyday things are fit for kings.

Lovely Bread and Butter Sandwiches

Cut thin slices of bread. Use only the very best butter. Like the White Rabbit. But don't put it in your watch like he did. Put it on the bread. Whip it first. So it will spread nicely. Put two buttered slices together. Trim off crusts. Cut from corner to corner. Place on square of foil. Wrap carefully. Make one for each person. Place on baking sheet in moderate oven. About 10 minutes. Serve "gift wrapped" in foil.

Santascones

Sift together 2 cups flour, 1 teaspoon salt, 5 teaspoons sugar, 3 teaspoons baking powder. With your fingertips (*wash* your hands!) rub 4 tablespoons butter into this. Beat 2 eggs, add 1/2 cup cream and pour into the flour mixture. Stir. On a lightly floured board, (*did* you wash your hands?) pat it out about 1/2 inch thick. Cut in fancy shapes. Brush tops with egg white. Bake on cookie sheet in moderate oven 12 to 15 minutes. Serve with jam and marmalade.

Very good with spiced tea and gossip. Grandmama and Mother. Not you.

AUNTY IS COMING TO TEA

Get all dressed up. It's a tea party. Just like Alice in Wonderland. Serve Aunty —

Tiddleywink Tea and Toast

Mix ½ cup sugar, ¼ cup orange juice and grated orange rind. Remove crusts from 6 slices of bread. Cut from corner to corner. Toast and butter these triangles. Spread with orange mixture. Place on cookie sheet in moderate oven until tops brown slightly.

or

Cut Christmas shapes from toast. Use cookie cutters. In center of each, put a dab of red jelly. Strawberry, raspberry, cranberry — whatever Mother has on hand. Sprinkle confectioner's sugar on top, like snow.

Cambric Tea. Use Mother's best teapot and black tea. No green, please. Put hot milk in a pitcher. Don't forget the sugar bowl. Now the tray. And napkins — maybe cloth ones? Toast is buttery.

Politely pour for Aunty. First, a half cup of hot milk. Then add hot tea. But *slowly*. Would she like sugar? Onelumportwo? Pass the toast. Then fix your own cup. Just like Aunty's.

PANCAKES FOR PAPA

Surprise Papa with pancakes. Use a packaged mix. Pour cooking oil in skillet or griddle. Put over a moderate heat. Pour large spoonful of batter for each cake. When it bubbles, turn to brown other side.

Warm the oven. Spread pancakes on a towel. Don't stack them. When Papa is ready, stack them on a warm plate. Serve with crisp bacon or grilled sausages.

try something different

Roll a sausage in each pancake. Serve with syrup, applesauce, apple butter or orange marmalade. Fried apple slices are good, too.

RESCUE FOR A RAINY DAY

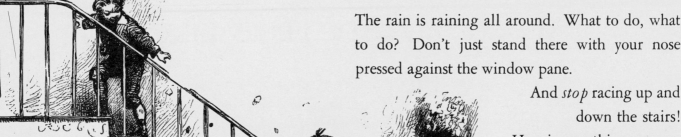

The rain is raining all around. What to do, what to do? Don't just stand there with your nose pressed against the window pane.

And *stop* racing up and down the stairs! Here is something you can make. And easy, too.

Humbug Hash

Line a square pan with waxed paper. Snip 12 big marshmallows into little pieces. Use kitchen shears dipped in flour. Break or chop 1 cup of nuts. Any kind will do. Melt 1 pound milk chocolate in double boiler. Pour half the chocolate in the pan. Sprinkle with nuts and marshmallows. Pour the rest of the chocolate on top. Let it cool. Break into pieces.

If Mother is tired from writing Christmas cards, why don't you fix your own lunch? See page 37.

WHEN MOTHER FEELS BRAVE

A taffy pull, what else? A good old-fashioned taffy pull. First, pull *yourself* together, Mother. And remember, grease all hands round. Smocks or aprons might help.

Ticky-Tacky Taffy

Over low heat, combine 1¼ cups sugar, 1½ teaspoons butter, 2 tablespoons mild vinegar, ¼ cup water. Stir until sugar dissolves. Then cook quickly until a small bit dropped in a cup of cold water forms a hard ball. Add ½ teaspoon vanilla. Pour this sticky mess onto a marble slab. Is Grandmother's marble-topped Victorian table in the living room? Be sure to *stay in the kitchen* and use a greased platter instead.

Is it cool enough to handle? Poke it with your finger. Does the hole stay? If so, pick it up. Make it into a ball. Then pull. And pull. And pull.

If you can keep this up, it will turn light and bubbly. When it does, stretch what isn't on the floor or in somebody's hair into a long, thin rope. Cut it in small pieces. Store in a box with a tight lid. Now, wasn't that fun?

On second thought, why don't you go have a Party in the Playroom? Turn the page.

A PARTY IN THE PLAYROOM

Plan a party in the playroom. Will you ask your Best Friend? Dolls like parties too. So do Teddy bears. And pets.

Fix some very easy things. And some things small enough for dolls and Teddy bears to eat.

Dolly's Lollypops

Stick toothpicks in gumdrops. Dip quickly in milk. Roll in powdered sugar.

Cookie Cakes

Mix 1 package cream cheese, ¼ cup milk, ¼ teaspoon sugar. Spread on 16 chocolate cookies. Put 4 cookies together, one on top of the other. You've made 4 layer cakes.

Tin Soldier Tarts

Do you have tart shells or patty shells? If not, fix make-believe shells. Cut 2 circles from white bread. Cut small hole in one circle. Put on top of other piece. Spread with butter and brown sugar. Toast. Fill with fruit. Top with whipped cream.

Jack Frosted Lemonade

Dip rims of glasses in water, then in powdered sugar. Fill with lemonade.

FOR THE BIRDS

Feed your feathered friends in winter. They will sing for you all summer long.

Keep regular bird feeders full of seed. Because it's Christmas time, try something new.

Little yellow goldfinches like sunflower seeds. They sing "Per-snick-ity, per-snick-ity!" Orioles like half an orange. The house finch loves cherries. So do robins. Red-headed woodpeckers call "Queer! Queer!" And it *is* queer, too. Because they like boiled potatoes.

The big, bold, black and yellow evening grosbeaks like nut meats. And cranberries.

Orioles will nest in your trees next summer if you put horsehair high on the hedges. They weave their nests with it. If you don't know a friendly horse with a long tail, string will do. Suet tied on a tree will bring many birds. And so will corn. And so will this —

Father's Fancy Finch Feeder

Use a piece of wood at least a foot long. Leave the bark on, if you like. Ask Father to screw a sturdy ring on one end. Can he drill several holes down and around? Big enough to hold small paper cups? Fill these cups with several mixtures. Suet and bird seed. Suet and nut meats. Suet and peanut butter. Put cups in holes.

Hang your Finch Feeder near a window. But not where cats can climb. Then watch the rosy finches feed on Father's Fancy Finch Feeder.

Isn't Father wonderful?

GOODIES FOR GRANDPAPA

When Grandpapa comes visiting, fix him a special treat.

Cinnamon Toasties

Toast day-old bread. Cut out fancy holiday shapes with cookie cutters. Butter them. Sprinkle with sugar and cinnamon. Put them on a cookie sheet in moderate oven until butter melts.

or

Cut day-old bread in narrow strips. Dip in melted butter. Roll in mixture of brown sugar, confectioner's sugar, cinnamon and dash of nutmeg. Place on cookie sheet in hot oven until toasted — about 5 minutes. So watch carefully.

Christmas Coffee

Melt 1 square of chocolate (1 ounce) in top of double boiler. Add ¼ cup sugar, dash of salt, 2 cups boiling water. Stir about 5 minutes. Pour in 1 cup milk and cream, mixed. Don't let it boil. Add a teaspoon vanilla extract and 2 cups hot coffee. Before you serve this, remember to whip the mixture with a fork.

For a cold drink — pour Christmas Coffee over a pint of vanilla ice cream. Use Mother's electric mixer and a big bowl. When it's whipped, pour in tall glasses. Maybe a peppermint candy cane in each one? Use it for a stirrer.

If Mother is tired from Christmas shopping, why don't you fix your own lunch? See page 37.

BREAKFAST FOR A TIRED MOTHER

You may do this all by yourself — and surprise Mother.

First, get out the tray. Then a plate. You'll need cup and saucer, knife, fork and spoon. Don't forget the salt and pepper. Does Mother use cream and sugar? Oh, yes — a napkin.

Decorate it with a sprig of evergreen. Maybe a small tree ornament? Whatever you think will make it pretty for Mother.

Now

Does she like juice? Orange, tomato, grapefruit, tangerine, prune, apple — What do you have on hand? Cranberry juice mixed with pineapple juice tastes good and it looks gay and Christmasy.

Put water on to boil for tea or instant coffee.

Scrambled Eggsactly

Eggs must be scrambled eggsactly to taste good. Break 2 eggs into bowl. Beat with fork. Add 2 tablespoons rich cream. Beat again. Melt 1 tablespoon butter in frying pan. Pour in eggs. Stir over *low* heat. Do they look thick? They're done. Or — surprise Mother with a One-Eyed Egg Sandwich. Look on the next page for the recipe.

One-Eyed Egg Sandwich

Break an egg in a small dish.

Use a round cookie or biscuit cutter. Cut a hole in center of a slice of bread. Butter both sides. Put it in a greased frying pan. When one side browns, turn it over. Now, careful! Slide egg into hole in bread. Turn heat down. Cover pan. Wait. Now peek inside. Has the white set? Then it's done. Use pancake turner to lift the One-Eyed Egg Sandwich. Carefully put it on Mother's plate.

Don't forget the coffee. Or is it tea?
Maybe cocoa? Ready now. Carry the tray to
Mother. When Mother has finished, take
the tray back to the kitchen. Stack the dishes. Tidy.
And don't forget to turn off the stove.

Won't Mother be surprised!

WHAT SHALL I DO NOW?

"Happy is the child who has inherited a garret full of old trunks, old furniture, old pictures, any kind of old things," wrote Mrs. M. E. W. Sherwood in her book, "The Art of Entertaining," printed 1892. "Do not deluge children with costly gifts. Capital scrap-books can be made by children. Old railway guides may be the foundation."

Now, you may not have a garret or an old railway guide handy. But you *can* make one thing Mrs. Sherwood wrote about in 1892. And make it better.

"It would be a great amusement for weeks before Christmas," she wrote, "if children were taught to make ornaments for the tree . . ."

Christmas Cones

Spray-paint ice cream cones. The pointy kind. Paint them gold, silver, frosty white, whatever you like. Let dry. Spread glue on rim of cone. Gently press a Christmas tree ball into cone. Put it hanger-side down. So just the round top will show. Like a dip of shiny ice cream.

Decorate with glitter. Tie ribbon or gold cord for hanging on tree.

Victorian Cornucopia

Cut 2 squares of heavy gift-wrap paper. Each one a different design and color. Glue back to back. Tape edges with colored tape if you like. Turn this square so that one corner points to your left hand and one corner points to your right. Roll left corner over to meet right corner, forming horn. Staple or tape together.

Decorate inside and out with parts of lace-paper doilies, braid, cut-outs from old Christmas cards. Stick a hole on each side. Tie gold cord through these to make a handle. Hang on the tree.

Fill some with popcorn or light weight candies. Leave some empty and paste pictures of old fashioned Santas or Christmas scenes inside.

Does Mother need a pretty table decoration? Or maybe a holder for Christmas cards? Make a very large cornucopia. Put it flat on the table. Decorate with fancy ribbon, bows or artificial flowers. Fill with tree ornaments or cards.

A GIFT IS SOMETHING YOU MAKE

When it's half-past November, gifts *should* be finished and ready to wrap.

Pomander Balls

These spicy-scented fancies were hung in linen closets, onceuponatime. Place unpeeled apple on pie tin. Stick in whole cloves. *Very* gently. All over. The more, the better. Roll it in 3 teaspoons ground cinnamon. Bake in a warm oven about 3 hours. When it cools, wrap in a scrap of lace, net or nylon stocking. Tie with ribbon. Leave long ends for hanging. Does Mother have an old bonnet with flowers? Use those for decoration.

Potpourri

Great Grandmother used a special china potpourri jar. Any screw-top jar will do. Remove petals from fresh roses. Spread on a screen. Put in a warm place until brittle. Pack in loose layers. To each layer, add allspice, cloves, nutmeg, cinnamon. Does lavender grow in your garden? Dry and add that. Paint the jar lid. Decorate it with decals. When snow is falling and skies are dreary, open your Rose Jar. Does it smell like summer and a sunny garden?

For other gifts to make, see pages 13, 25 and 34.

New Year's Resolution: Start making gifts at a quarter to June.

A WINTER PICNIC

When it's cold and snowy outside, isn't it nice by the fire? Could you plan a winter picnic round the hearth?

First, ask Mother. Tell her you'll put a drip catcher on the floor. *Not* newspapers. Maybe an old plastic tablecloth? Or a big beach towel? Always put up the fire screen. And don't start the fire yourself.

Ask Father to lay a good, long-lasting fire. He's an expert at this. He knows you never burn charcoal inside the house. He uses hardwood. So watch how he does it. Isn't Father wonderful?

Wait until part of the fire glows. Like Rudolph the Reindeer's red nose. That's best for cooking. Is there a water pistol hidden somewhere? You can use it for flare-ups. That's *all*. Just flare-ups. The ones in the fire. On second thought, maybe you'd better use a clothes sprinkler instead. You must keep your mind on your cooking.

Now, even though it's winter, this is going to be the very essence of a picnic. Because all the recipes begin with "S." That makes sense, doesn't it?

Choose between Shish-Ke-Bobbles and Shush Puppies. Between Somersault Salad and Stuffed Sellery. S'Mores for dessert. Pour S'Milk in a glass. 'Sterrific? Sertainly. 'SChristmas, too.

ROUND THE HEARTH

Shish-Ke-Bobbles

Use regular barbecue skewers. Or ask Father to straighten several unpainted coat hangers. Use pot holders. Cut beef in 1-inch chunks. Put in pottery bowl. Pour this mixture over it: $\frac{1}{2}$ cup olive oil, $\frac{1}{2}$ cup wine vinegar, $\frac{1}{4}$ teaspoon salt, dash of fresh-ground black pepper, 1 clove crushed garlic. If you like, add pinch rosemary, oregano, thyme, bay leaf, dash onion salt, or 2 cloves. Place in ice box 2 to 3 hours.

Continued

Continued

On the skewer, put a chunk of beef, a Tiny Tim tomato, a Mighty Mushroom and a square of green pepper. Grill over glowing logs.

Shush Puppies

These are pampered pups in a poke, gift wrapped in aluminum foil. Put hot-dog roll on square of foil. Spread with butter and mustard. Place slice of cheese on this. Then the hot dog. Now a spoonful of relish. Wrap it carefully in the foil. Make one Shush Puppy for each picnic person. Store in ice box until ready to heat and eat. Then place on cookie sheet. Bake in 375° oven 12 minutes.

Somersault Salad

In a bowl, tear lettuce into bite-sized pieces. Chop green pepper, cucumber, chives (or green tops of little onions) and add. Then add slices of avocado. Crumble blue cheese over all. When ready to serve, pour on Italian style salad dressing. Not too much. Just enough to lightly coat the leaves, after you toss them over, and over, and over. With a wooden fork and spoon, of course.

Stuffed Sellery

Cut celery in 2-inch pieces. Stuff cream cheese in hollow part. Sprinkle paprika on it.

S'Mores

These are called S'Mores because they always make you want some more. On a graham cracker, put 4 squares of plain milk chocolate candy bar. Toast 2 marshmallows. When they're gooey, push them onto the chocolate. Top with another cracker.

HELPFUL HANDS

Tie ribbons on the candy canes. String cranberries and popcorn. Write thank-you notes. Or try this.

Backdoor Decoration

Use an evergreen branch. One that fits the door. Spray ends of branch with snow. Or dab ends of needles and pine cones with colorless nail polish. Sprinkle with glitter. Tie on candy canes and small ornaments. Maybe little toys and dolls? Or cut out cardboard gingerbread boys and girls. Paint them. Dress them up with braid and sequins. Hang up your branch with a big red ribbon. Now the back door is as pretty as the front door. Maybe prettier?

If Mother is tired from putting up decorations, why don't you fix your own lunch?
See page 37.

GAIETY FOR GROWNUPS

Grownups like parties, too. Ask if you can have some of the goodies for your own party in the playroom. First, help mother fix these.

Fix and Freeze Fancies

Cut crusts from day-old bread. Butter. Cut in fancy shapes. Toast on cookie sheet. Spread with —

Cream Cheese: Add dash of salt, paprika, onion juice. Decorate with minced parsley.

Deviled Ham: Add a little mayonnaise, lemon juice. Decorate with slice of olive.

Hard-boiled Egg: Chop fine. Add salt, pepper, paprika, Worcestershire, dash of Tabasco, curry powder. Decorate with pimiento or sprig of parsley.

Place on cookie sheet. Freeze.
Pack 24 to a box.
Thaw 30 minutes before serving.

Day-Ahead Delights

Precious Prunes: Soak large prunes overnight. Drain, remove pits, fill with chutney. Wrap in bacon, fasten with toothpicks, store in icebox. At party time, broil until bacon crisps.

continued

Vegetable Dip: Mix half sour cream, half mayonnaise. Add grated onion, Worcestershire, dry mustard, chives, horseradish, salt and black pepper.

Curried Nuts: Heat in skillet $\frac{1}{4}$ cup olive oil, 1 tablespoon curry powder, 1 tablespoon Worcestershire. Add 2 cups pecans or walnuts. Stir until coated. Pour into baking pan lined with brown paper. Bake at 300° until crisp.

Last Minute Goodies

Mix sour cream and red caviar, spread on thin pumpernickel.
Put blue cheese on round cracker, top with cucumber, dab of anchovy paste.
Spread any cheese on saltines, sprinkle with any seasoned salt, paprika. Broil.

Desperate Devices

Are there more guests than Mother planned on? Never mind. Try these.
Spread bite-sized shredded wheat on cookie sheet. Sprinkle with onion or garlic salt. Broil.

Spread potato chips on cookie sheet. Sprinkle with grated cheese and onion salt. Broil until bubbly.

Spread any cheese between any nut halves.

Sprinkle Parmesan cheese over hot popcorn.

If Mother is tired from making these goodies, why don't you fix your lunch? See page 37.

YULETIDE SUPPER

This time of the year is the nicest. Evening comes early. The world outside turns lavender blue. From your lighted windows, golden squares splash across the snow.

And inside, in all the houses, it's toasty warm and bright. And the smell of evergreens and cookies baking mix with the sounds of laughter and scampering about.

Soon, the candles will be lighted. And everyone will settle down for a holiday supper by candlelight.

Soup of the Evening

Cook 1 medium onion, chopped fine in 2 tablespoons butter. Stir in 1 tablespoon flour, 1 teaspoon salt, $\frac{1}{2}$ teaspoon celery salt. Blend in $\frac{1}{2}$ cup peanut butter. Gradually stir in 2 cups milk. Stir until mixture thickens. Add 2 cups tomato juice. Bring just to a boil. Serves 4.

Golden Casserole

Grease a casserole dish. Put in a layer of sausages. Sprinkle with brown sugar, lemon juice. Over this, put a layer of canned peeled apricots. Sprinkle with brown sugar, lemon juice. Repeat until casserole is full. Bake uncovered in moderate oven. Serve with mashed potatoes. Sh-h-h! the quick kind. In a box. And asparagus. The quick kind. In a can. Or maybe string beans?

BY CANDLELIGHT

Cranberry Ham

If you have no sausages, try this. In saucepan, heat ½ cup whole, canned cranberry sauce, ½ teaspoon dry mustard, ⅛ teaspoon ground cloves, ½ teaspoon cinnamon, 1 tablespoon vinegar. Stir until mixture comes just to a boil. Pour this over 3 or 4 cups cubed, baked ham in casserole. Heat in low oven. Serves 4.

Baked Apples

Make ahead. Serve warm or cold.
With sugar and rich cream.
First, wash and dry apples. Take
out the cores. Put apples in
baking dish. Fill place where cores
were with brown sugar and
butter. Pour water into dish. Cover.
Bake about 45 minutes at 375°.
Can you stick them with a fork?
Then they're done.

And after Supper?
How about a story hour with
Dickens' *Christmas Carol?*
And — so to bed.

SERENDIPITY SALADS

Say seh-ren-dipity. It means being able to find good things when you aren't really looking. In the fairy tale, three Princes of Serendip were always finding wonderful things by chance — a happy accident.

These salads were happy accidents. Why not make up your own serendipity salads.

Christmas Candle Salad

Put crisp lettuce leaf on plate. Then a slice of pineapple. Peel banana. Cut in half. Set this in the pineapple hole for a make-believe candle.
Stick a cherry on top with a toothpick.

Snow Man Salad

Put half a canned pear on lettuce leaf. Cover it with cottage cheese. If it won't spread, add a little mayonnaise. Use raisins for eyes, nose and buttons. A cinnamon red hot for the mouth.

LONG AGO LEFTOVERS

Here are two foods from long ago. One from the North.
One from the South.

Snow Ice Cream

When leaves turned red in the fall, Vermont men went into the forest. They gathered
sap from maple trees. Indians showed them how. Then they made maple syrup and
sugar. Sometimes they poured a cupful on a snow bank — an old-time ice cream
sundae. You can do this today. Wait for a storm to bring fresh, clean snow.

Hoecake

In the South, people who worked in the fields cooked corn-meal cake over open fires.
On a hoe. So can you. All you need is a clean hoe, a good fire and loving parents.
Ask them before you try. You *may* have to wait for summer.

In a bowl, mix 1 cup corn meal, $\frac{1}{2}$ teaspoon salt, 1 tablespoon bacon grease. Pour in
a little boiling water. Just enough to hold it together. Pat it into 2 thin cakes. Small
enough to fit the hoe — one at a time.

You *can* bake them in a well-greased, heated iron pan. In a preheated oven. 375°
for about 30 minutes. Serve hot.

In 1776 Benjamin Franklin wrote that hoecake was better than a Yorkshire muffin.
What do you think?

If Mother is tired from writing letters to Santa, why don't you fix your own lunch? *See page 37.*

A PICNIC FOR YOUR PETS

You're nice to your pets all year round. So why not plan a picnic for them? Just because it's Christmas.

Snow Ball Cupcakes

Cut a hole in top of ready-made cupcakes. Put a small scoop of vanilla ice cream in it.

Animal Frosties

Put 2 vanilla wafers together with ready-made frosting — whatever flavor Mother has on hand. Spread it on top, too. Stand an animal cracker up in the frosting. Make several. Line them up. It's a circus parade.

Surprise! Why don't you eat all this yourself? Give your dog a dog biscuit. Cats like ice cream. Birds like a small slice of apple. Rabbits really do like carrots. Fish like whatever you've been giving them out of that box of fish food.

And turtles — now, how do you have a picnic with a turtle? Well, Alice did. Of course, he *was* a Mock Turtle. And she had a kind of a picnic with a caterpillar, too. Anything is possible.

With a little love and kindness, every day is picnic day for pets.

CHRISTMAS COOKIES AND SUGAR PLUMS

Christmas goodies made by you are the nicest gifts. So don't eat them *all* up.

Krisp Kringles

Mix 2 cups flour, 1 cup powdered sugar, 1 cup cornstarch. Cream 1 pound butter. Stir while you add flour mixture slowly to butter. Divide in 4 parts. Wrap in foil. Chill. Shape in 1-inch balls. (Did you wash your *hands?*) Place 2 inches apart on ungreased cookie sheet. Flatten with floured fork. Bake at 325° about 20 minutes or until lightly browned. 7 dozen.

Paint gay, holiday designs on plain cookies before you bake them. Mix 1 egg yolk with 1 teaspoon water. Put in muffin cups. Add food coloring. Use small brushes or toothpicks.

Marshmallow Delights

Melt chocolate in 1 double boiler, caramel in another. Quickly dip marshmallows, roll in chopped nuts. Use toothpicks; or dip the marshmallows in bowl of cream, roll in piles of colored sugar.

Christmas Chuckles

It's hard to tell if these are cookies or candy. Boil ½ cup white corn syrup, 1 package butter-scotch bits, ½ cup sugar. Turn off heat. Add ¾ cup peanut butter, 3 cups crushed cornflakes. Drop spoonfuls on waxed paper.

Honeypops

Put 3 quarts *popped* corn in large bowl. Boil 1 cup honey, 1 cup sugar, dash of salt. It's done when small bit dropped in cup of cold water makes soft ball. Stir popcorn while you pour this in. Grease your hands (you're *sure* you washed them?) squeeze into balls. Makes more than 2 dozen.

Tree Cookies

Would you like to hang decorated cookies on your Christmas tree? Use your favorite recipe for rolled cookies. Before baking, poke hole near the edge of cookie. Put a dry bean in the hole. Remove bean very carefully, when cookies cool. String on bright ribbons.

If Mother is just tired, why don't you fix your own lunch? See page 37.

WHY NOT FIX YOUR OWN LUNCH?

Spread peanut butter on bread. Put slice of ham in between.

Spread peanut butter on bread. Put canned cranberry jelly in between.

Spread peanut butter on date-nut bread. Put cream cheese in between.

Spread peanut butter on orange-nut bread. Put honey in between.

Spread peanut butter on bread. Put deviled ham in between.

Spread peanut butter on rye bread. Put crisp bacon in between.

Spread peanut butter on whole wheat bread. Put cheddar cheese in between.

Spread peanut butter on bread. Put grape jelly in between.

Spread peanut butter on bread. Put mayonnaise and lettuce in between.

Spread peanut butter on Boston brown bread. Put apple butter in between.

Spread peanut butter on cinnamon toast.

Spread peanut butter on corn bread. Put slice of chicken in between.

Spread peanut butter on stone-ground white bread. Put orange marmalade in between.

Spread peanut butter on crackers. Top with marshmallow. Broil.

Spread peanut butter on bread. Put mayonnaise and sliced bananas in between.

Did You Know You Could Make Your Own Peanut Butter?

For every cup of peanuts, use $1\frac{1}{2}$ to 3 tablespoons vegetable oil. If nuts are unsalted, add about $\frac{1}{2}$ teaspoon salt for each cup. Put in electric blender. This won't keep as long as the ready-made kind. Do you care?

THE KETTLEDRUM

Afternoon tea started in England. Some say the Princess of Wales began it. In the 1870's it was called a Kettledrum. Why?

Because at tea parties in Victorian England people talked so fast and so loud, they sounded like a kettledrum. The most rattling of all drums.

That's what Mrs. John Sherwood wrote in her book called "Manners and Social Usages." It was printed in 1884, when Victoria was queen of England. So Mrs. Sherwood ought to know.

Afternoon tea parties are nicer now. But the tea is worse. Because it takes time to make good tea. And people hurry so much today. Queen Victoria *never* hurried.

Do you want to learn how to make good tea? As good as in Queen Victoria's time? Well, never *mind*. Read this anyway.

Tea is divided into black and green tea. Then there's an in between tea. *That's* called oolong. Forget about oolong. It'll be too long before you like oolong. So — so long, oolong.

In an enamel kettle, heat water *fresh* from the tap. Put hot water in china or pottery teapot. This warms the teapot. Put tea in tea ball. One teaspoon for each cup. And "one for the pot." When water boils and is dancing all over, it's ready. Empty teapot.

continued

OR AFTERNOON TEA

Put tea ball in it. Pour boiling water in it. Tea leaves have oil. Keep it safe for good taste. So put lid on pot fast as you can.

Let tea steep 3 to 5 minutes. Take out tea ball. Cover teapot with tea cosy. This is a sort of padded helmet. It keeps the tea warm. It *ought* to keep it hot. But it doesn't.

Pour tea into thin, white china cups. Serve black tea with milk. Green tea with lemon. Black tea in the morning. Green tea after noon. Oolong in between.

There, now. Wasn't that easy?

Just remember — Queen Victoria was very fond of tea. And she was *very* fond of Santa Claus. And any friend of Santa Claus ought to be a friend of yours.

Especially at this time of year —